Blasphemer

Blasphemer

Bill Yarrow

To Jacob,

stay blasphemous,
my friend!

with admiration,

Bill

(5.29.15)

Brothers K

ISBN: 978-1-943170-01-2

Cover Image: Bill Yarrow "Telamon on the Nevsky Prospekt"
Cover Design: Jane L. Carman
Interior Design: Bonnie Boyd
Production Director: Jane L. Carman

Typefaces: Garamond and News Gothic

Published by: Lit Fest Press / Festival of Language

Carman
688 Knox Road 900 North
Gilson, Illinois 61436

festivalwriter.org

for Leah

Table of Contents

Part One: To Blaspheme or Not to Blaspheme

Part Two: Blasphemy? I Know Not Blasphemy

Part Three: To Pluck Out the Heart of My Blasphemy

Part Four: This Above All: To Thine Own Self, Be Blasphemous

Part Five: Get Thee to a Blasphemer

Part Six: The Rest is Blasphemy

Part One:

To Blaspheme or Not to Blaspheme

Eyes off the Road

One by one I lost my desires.
Dirty ambition left first.
Knowledge raged but then it cooled.
Riches never had the hook very deep.
Achievement uncoupled from success seemed pointless.
Friendship became recursive.
Appetite lost its urgency.
Form declined into artifice.
Love stopped feeding me so I stopped feeding it.
Insight evaporated when memory left.
Lust lingered longest.

My desires, gaily arrayed, bolted to a
lapis slab, await me in Heaven.
With any luck I'll go to Hell.

JOAN OF DARK

What happens in heaven stays in heaven.
"That's not true," she said to me. "You know
it's not true." Yes, the acts of paradise,
slippery like syrup, slide down the clouds
and drip onto the tops of the trees where
birds and squirrels reveal them to man.
"What color are the birds?" she asked. Pink.
Pink birds and checkerboard squirrels
reveal the sly doings of the chubby cherubs.
"What's sly doings?" I meant "sky" doings.
Reveal the sky doings of half-pint angels.
"I love heaven, don't you?" I'm not allowed to
tell. They will burn me at the stake if I tell.
"Like Joan of Dark?" Just like Joan of Dark.

Bill Yarrow

How Religion Got Its Start

One little kid. One little kid.
My father sold me for two zuzim.
One little kid.

/ /

One little kid. One little kid.
For two zuzim, my father sold me
to terrorists. They tied me up.
One little kid.

/ /

One little kid. One little kid.
Terrorists tied me up with explosives
and sat me on the road.
One little kid.

/ /

One little kid. One little kid.
Tied with explosives. On the road. In the sun.
One little kid blanching in the sun.

/ /

One little kid. One little kid.
Goats came and ate the bombs.
Ate all the bombs.

/ /

Time passed and ate the goats, ate all the goats.

///////////////////////////

///////////////////////////

In the bearded sun, I see a golden goat.
On his back rides a shining boy.
He is the Realignment and the Knife.

Bill Yarrow

ABRAHAM

I came late to sunrise. The hills were lit
with goats. Everything shimmered in
small steps. I closed my eyes.

The Kinneret sits back in its water
waiting to be made to shine.
My blood is like the sea.

Jerusalem against the sun. People
draw lots for the shadows
and put down spears.

I walk toward walls.
The late sun enters my skin
like the blade of Isaac's knife.

Kinneret: Sea of Galilee.

HOLY WEEK

you in Gurnee
watching the attacks
on television

I in Seville
the plaza filled with scourges
in the hands of hooded men

you in the sun room
contemplating the clematis
as it climbs the garage

I opposite the bright cathedral
contemplating God
in all His disguises

one day I will take you to Grenada
and you will see
how beautiful the Alhambra is

Bill Yarrow

Ribs

Man reached in the carcass of the Lord
and tore Satan from the rib of God.
The mountains of humility went silent,
the rain of regency dried its eyes,
and the clouds of unknowing began to know.
Snow masquerading as kindness ballooned
into bombast as the world washed its hands
of worldliness. Then indifference, stiff as a
wombat penis, stirred and woke from the dream
of cascading penury. I am imbricated by the
slabs of dead ideas. I am teased by vaults of
no gold. Ghosts hold me to votes I disavow.
There is a formidable hole in the latent sky.
It takes all my strength not to worship it.

Ratatouille

"The good years shall devour them."

—*King Lear* Act V, sc iii

The body receives its embrace but
only by the anti-body. Effete angels, stoic
guardians of suffering, circled by the birds
of perpetration, look on in translucent hopelessness.
Spurred on by anesthetists, I fall on the mercy of the corpse.

The world enforces the larceny of living. A widow vacations
in the Alps, falls in love with her concierge. Across
a desert, a Bengali widower walks a crooked mile.
Bring spices, an incensed container, and, for
the sacrifice, a decorated carving knife.

Bill Yarrow

Car Alarm

Wires shot.
Timing's off.
Plugs and points
need to be replaced.
Gaskets smashed.
Hoses rotted.
That's the body for you.
Most mornings won't start.
Dings, nicks, and scratches
on the exterior. Failing
internal combustion organs.
God the mechanic
is a little booked up.
He'll see you after you're dead.

Jesus! I hate poems like this!

Kimchi Hatchet

She shouldn't have trusted her townhome
to the apple-shaped developer because now look:

she's got ants with white wings in her cabinets.
"Oh, my God!" she shrieks from her apron.

You need a hug, he tells her and opens
his arms. She declines the embrace.

"You're not Jesus, you know. No matter
how much you think you wanna be."

Bill Yarrow

GETTING GODLESS

I.
- God is man squared. That is to say, God is man raised to a higher power.
- Man is the root, the square root, of God.
- We believe in the ideal (truth, wisdom, justice, honor, integrity, selflessness, sacrifice, compassion, goodness) and God is the name we give to that ideal.
- What else is God but a heuristic for what we want to do with our lives?
- The worship of God is the worship of perfection. The perfection of space: infinity. The perfection of time: eternity. The perfection of power: omnipotence. The perfection of knowledge: omniscience. The perfection of behavior: virtue.
- Since the Fall, falling is what we've learned to do.
- We are blemished perfections.
- Man is the asymptote of what he predicates God to be.
- We define ourselves by what we are trying not to be. Some men try to be men by not being womanly. Some women try to be women by not being manly. Some men try to be men by not being too manly. Some women try to be women by not being too womanly. People assert their humanness by differentiating it from brutishness. Man posits God's divinity in contradistinction to humanity.
- Science teaches us that there is no one thing in the world, that everything is made of smaller and smaller substances. God's indivisibility draws a line in the sand against science.
- Dostoyevsky said that without God, everything is permitted. Behind that statement is the correct notion that with God, anything can be prohibited.
- God can be seen in man's ability to imagine God.

II.
- We don't buy into God; we marry into Him.
- Agnosticism: a philosophical position built not on belief or doubt but on an inability to decide.
- An agnostic is a tepid thing, a spineless thing, a mushy thing.
- The deists were atheists without the courage of their convictions.
- Modern religion: carpe deism.
- The atheist can't stop thinking about God. The religious man can't stop thinking about atheism.

- The second millennium was a fight for freedom of religion. The third millennium will be a fight for freedom from religion.

III.
- Jealousy is a cocktail made of equal parts insecurity and possession.
- Before we can be jealous, we must make our mate our thing.
- *Our God is a jealous God.* What an unfortunate idea.
- The God fantasy infantilizes man.
- Is God smiling or is God frowning? That's what every religious war's about, wanting God to be happy.
- Suggestiveness is not a god.
- Religion scares the hell out of me when I see it scaring hell into everyone else.
- Religion isn't about spirituality—it's about ritual.
- What begins as respect ends as worship.
- Religion is division.

IV.
- Amulets. Lucky charms. God.
- Overseers. Consciences. God.
- Kings. Fathers. God.
- Policemen. Judges. God.
- Teachers. Authors. God.
- Accountants. Engineers. God.
- God—the Great Excuse.
- God—the Seatbelt of the Soul.
- Personal trainers. Personal bankers. Personal gods.
- God: a godforsaken construct.
- Heraclitus for God.

V.
- Vengeance is mine, saith the Lord. God is Love. Same God.
- The Lord will rain for ever and ever, and, on that day, the Earth shall be wet and His name wet.
- The reason magic tricks look real to us is that we are desperate to believe in

something, but there's nothing to believe in.

- Embrace sham. Squeeze tight. It'll shatter and the world will be honest again.
- Numerology derives its meaning from manipulation. Like magic, it's entrancing but no less deceiving.
- Spirituality is a shell game.

VI.

- The divine is our great wish, but there's nothing objective about a wish.
- Prayer is an affirmation of belief, but prayer as an expectation of response is absurd *beyond belief.*
- Wishes are not real, but wishing is real. Dreams are not real, but dreaming is real. Thoughts are not real, but thinking is real. Belief is not real, but believing is real. The world is full of wishes, dreams, thoughts, and beliefs embodied, made real.
- As Jesus embodies sacrifice, as Buddha embodies renunciation, so God embodies meaning.
- I am the dream of my parents embodied. Everyone is a dream made real.
- There is no difference in effect between false belief and true belief. The effect of any belief is always tangible.
- What is efficacious in belief systems is not the object of the belief (i.e. Jesus or Buddha) but belief itself.
- God is a cosmic placebo.
- Reality exists independent of our perception of it, but reality does not exist *for us* independent of our perception of it.

VII.

- A religious leader is a vanity mirror for his congregation.
- Religion exists to oppose the incursions of time.
- Occasionally, a saint can beat the odds, but, in the long run, the house always wins. Who lives in the house? The devil.
- Christian morality is a geometry, a drawing of lines. Judaism with its rounded fences is a calculus; it wants to measure the area under the curve. Everything else is string theory.
- The population of the world accepts unthinkingly the rightness of the religion or the atheism it is born into.

- You want to worship an ideal (call it God), you want to believe it possible—go ahead. If it stretches you, if it makes you taller, great. Just don't smear it with the bullshit of personification and intentionality and intervention.

VIII.

- People are desperate to posit a soul—they need something to blame their good impulses on.
- The soul is a pilot light.
- Science's bio-chemical refutation of the mind/body split has killed the concept of the soul in man.
- No soul = no shame.
- If science really wants to understand spirituality and mysticism, it should begin by unraveling the phenomenon of *feeling* other people looking at us, the phenomenon of *feeling* the eyes of someone walking behind us on our necks.
- I don't believe in spirits or a spirit realm. I do, however, believe in thought. The brain is uncontained by the skull. Its waves leak out and interfere in the world. Ghosts, called spirits, are, more precisely, the coalescence of leaked thinking.
- Exhaustion of the body frees the mind to wander in the spirit.
- Soul—a comforting delusion.

IX.

- The person who eats his vegetables first is not morally superior to the person who eats his vegetables last.
- There's no virtue that can't be vulgarized.
- Depravity doesn't evolve; it mutates.
- Because goodness is fundamentally a function of will, virtue can never be habitual.
- Utility is always a value, but awareness isn't always a good.
- An ethics of expedience, not of obligation.
- There are accomplices to virtuous acts as well as to crimes. What, in basketball, is called an assist, in morality, is called virtuous complicity.
- Integrity, indistinguishable from intransigence or recalcitrance, is just a more exalted form of perversity.
- The moral man brings up phlegm but does not spit it out.

X.

- Cause murks morality.
- Relativism is the philosophical justification of deviance.
- To eliminate deviance, eliminate absolutes. For Dostoyevsky, the Absolute was indistinguishable from God.
- Morality is dependent on observation. God is watching, the police are watching, my neighbors are watching.
- If you want to construct a moral society, construct one where people are always in each other's presence.
- The smaller the community, the more moral it is.
- *I'm OK, you're OK* is the sniveling Laertes saying, *Exchange forgiveness with me, Hamlet.* I'll let you off the hook if you let me off the hook.
- Morality is not a quid pro quo. Morality is washing our own dirty backs. *You wash my back and I'll wash yours* is no different from *you wash my backside and I'll wash yours.* The only difference is, in the second instance, the disgusting nature of the transaction is made clearer.
- *Do unto others as you would have others do unto you.* Quid pro blowjob.
- Morality is a refraining from, not an indulging in.

XI.

- Understanding is dangerous because it results, inevitably, in forgiveness.
- Understanding is the secret tunnel that runs from the head directly to the heart. Forgiveness is a function of understanding.
- Empathy is denial of conscience, vilification of judgment.
- Empathy is a form of enabling. It says, Y*es, yes, yes! I know what you mean. I understand how you feel.* Empathy is part of the conspiracy of all ideas, all beliefs, all feelings being equal.
- Empathy results in exculpation. It results in: "O Doctor Mengele, you poor man!"
- Forgiveness is no virtue. It's the beginning of vice.

XII.

- Before genetics, there were gods.
- Gregor Mendel reinvented fate.
- The modern determinist gods are heredity, environment, and culture.
- Everyone alive is an exemplar of a triumphant fitness.
- The debate between Athens and Sparta was really a unified argument in

favor of nurture, in favor of the environment over heredity.

- What's providence for one person is deliberation for someone else. The Corinthian messenger's volition tastes like fate to Oedipus.
- Luck is the name we give to unwilled repetition.
- The crosses and the stars we wear—magic amulets—protect us from ourselves.
- Superstition is the name we give to the spurious cause of a legitimate effect.
- The greatest superstition is a belief in providence or grace.

XIII.

- Who invented virtue—I say the devil.
- Who invented coherence—I say the devil.
- Who invented pity—I say the devil.
- Who invented forgiveness—I say the devil.
- Who invented reward—I say the devil.
- Who invented hope—I say the devil.
- Who invented religion—I say the devil.
- Who invented the devil—religion.

Jesus, Zombie

"Jesus was a zombie?" I ask, shocked.
My uncle turns towards me with a look
of red surprise on his face. *Absolutely!*
He was the <u>King</u> of the Zombies. He was
one of the first to die and then come back
so he's among the <u>original</u> undead. Sly,
<u>very</u> crafty zombie, let me tell you—
gets people to eat <u>his</u> body and drink
<u>his</u> blood, and when they do, they belong
to him—<u>forever</u>! He not only eats their
brains, but he also devours their <u>hearts</u>,
and then they can <u>never</u> die. Watch out
for this Jesus fella, I tell you. He's <u>after</u>
you. And he'll <u>never</u> stop chasing you down.
"What'll I do if I see him?" I ask, shaking
in my chair. *Cross your fingers like this—*
that'll make him think you're one of them,
and he'll leave you be. "What lies are
you telling my boy?!" my dad shouts
running up from the basement. He grabs
Uncle Ned by his shirt, jerks him up,
and starts to choke him. *Hey, take it easy,*
brother! Just teaching the kid to fear the Lord.

DEAD PARENTAL UNITS

1.

Each death a sonnet, every grief
fourteen lines. Not yours. I refuse
you this thing. I sat next to you
in the hospital, your mouth open
on one side, your last breath escaped.
I connect you with no other
dead or myself with weeping sons.
I am only this son, holding
his father's dead hand, watching his
father's dead mouth. I will not write
you sonnets. Sonnets are boxes.
Spaces for pain. Graves to lie in.
Graves! I withhold your raw last line.

2.

Another death, another sonnet. Every
grief fourteen fucking lines. Not yours.
I stood next to you in my sister's house,
the family huddled around like reporters
at a tornado. Terrified, we watched you
drown. At dawn, they wheeled you out.
Yes, mothers die and sons are very sad,
but I am not one of the many. I am one
of the few who will not write you sonnets.
I'm sorry. Maybe that would have given
you...what? Solace? Satisfaction? Sonnets
are boxes. Coffins! You want me to build
you a coffin? How many do you need?

Bill Yarrow

ANTIGONE DÉTENTE

I'm that age, I guess. People keep asking me
what I want for my funeral. I don't give a shit.
Let the dogs lick my bones. Throw my ashes
out the window. If I die in the autumn, rake
the orange leaves over my arms. Sure, put my
clavicle on your mantel. Feel free to laminate
my lungs. Toss my heart off the dock. Use
me if you run out of dark molasses or caulk.
Make origami or a caftan or wicker furniture
or a raku pot of me. Tan my hide. Feed me
to rabid macaques. Dissolve me in nitric acid.
Water the garden of my face. Give Achilles
free reign to drag me through the mud. Don't
feel guilty. It's OK, really. I, Priam, absolve you.

So they asked his wife and daughters and sons
what they wanted for their father, and they said,
Bury the bastard. Serves him right for being glib.

Part Two:

Blasphemy? I Know Not Blasphemy

THERE'S NO CRYING IN POETRY

"There's no crying in poetry. There's
no crying in poetry!" says Coach
Bukowski, barnacle-gnarled,
stomping on the ground behind
third base. But the poetry pitcher
is crying, the poetry catcher is
sobbing, the poetry short stop is
bawling, the poetry center fielder
is doubled over, weeping bitterly.
Bukowski shakes his head. *Jesus,*
how the hell did I wind up here?
He yells, "Hey! There's no crying
in fucking poetry! Ya hear me?"
but no one on the poetry team
is listening.

But in the beer garden
across the street, the bar poets,
looking up, are waving gloves
at the ball sailing towards them.
They stretch their hands above
their heads and call out

"I got it!"

"No, I got it!"

"I said, I got it!"

Then they collide and lie like kinks in a
tangled hose. The ball lands and takes a
bad hop, hits the barmaid smack on the lip.
"Don't you cry. Don't you dare," she hears
Bukowski saying, and, though it really hurts,
and though she really wants to, she doesn't.

OVERHEARD AT THE OPEN MIC

"This poem is for my best friend who committed suicide last night."
"My girlfriend left me. I couldn't believe it either."
"You won't understand this poem, but I'm going to read it anyway."
"I'm not kidding: this *actually* happened to me."
"I'm not *really* a poet."
"Two more."

"You'll like this one; this one is funny."
"I bet I can shock you by saying the word 'shit.' "
"God healed my spirit."
"Pay attention: this one is deep."
"How beauteous is beauty!"
"Two more."

"My childhood was fun."
"My wife is a bitch, I mean goddess."
"This poem is a double villanelle in seven parts. Part One."
"My dad loved me, but he never told me he loved me. Fuckin' bastard!"
"I'm glad I decided to keep the baby."
"Two more."

"Men keep staring at my body. Here's a poem about that."
"I really like sex. Here's a poem about that."
"You've heard this one before, but I want to read it again."
"The Holocaust happened in my soul."
"The Muse gives good head."
"Two more."

"I spent last summer in the Côte d'Azur."
"This one is untitled."
"Nature is SO pretty!"
"I just *love* Jack Gilbert."
"I wrote this last night."
"Two more."
"Three more."
"Four more."

Bill Yarrow

A New Kind of Madness

in my youth I was enamored of the moon
—that is to say, lunacy

I applauded the bizarre in nature
I appropriated the gratuitous from dreams
I drank brashness and frenzy from books

what mad things I did!
(throwing a bucket of water on the naked couple in the bed)

what mad things I said!
(telling you your heart was filled with flies)

what mad things I wrote!
(what is the interstice of bliss he insisted)

then Thomas went mad and threw himself under a bus
then Liat hanged herself
then Miko couldn't stop laughing and died

so I became careful

I monitored my sadness
I governed my excitement
I trimmed all my excess
I ramped up my sensible brain

and now I am old and reminiscent
and like Funes I remember it all

Halloween in New Orleans
President's Day in Aberdeen
New Year's Eve in Prague

Thanksgiving in Atlanta
Easter in Bangalore

but in my visionary senescence
I am haunted by a new kind of madness
a dementia of time

mEmOrY   [[[unmoored ·from ·chronology]]]
Me ·Mo ·Ry   [[[stripped ·of ·its ·ardor]]]
<u>M</u> > <u>E</u> > <u>M</u> >>> <u>O</u>>>>>><u>R</u>>>>>> <u>Y</u>   [[[reduced ·to ·obtuseness]]]

THE NEW BLURB

"The old blurb is predictable in its praise and universally ignored."
—Martin San Romanese

1. This book touches your heart but not in a good way.

2. Every day I thank God that books like this are hard to find.

3. To give you a sense of how infectious this book is, after I read it I felt ill.

4. There's nothing that can be said about this book that hasn't already been said about some other book.

5. This is the just kind of book I never read and you should too.

6. This book does the work of imagination for you in that it is hard to imagine how it could be any worse.

7. If I truly understood all that's in this book, I would go mad and I don't have the insurance coverage for that.

8. I found this book, being not hard to write, very easy to ignore.

9. Don't let the fact that the writing in this book is terrible dissuade you from buying it. Support independent presses!

10. This book proves the truth of the falsehood: "Anyone can be a writer."

POETRY IS OTHER PEOPLE

I.   Is there nothing out there but misery?
       Tales of human fading? Nomenclatures
       of the fallen body? Even if we forbade
       the saddest subjects, the tornadoes
       would still be there, the typhoon,
       the mudslide, the angry snow squall,
       the red volcano, the bridge collapsing,
       the window crashing onto the sidewalk,
       the flames leaping from roof to roof,
       from car to car, from tree to tree,
       insolent and snickering, would still be there.

II.   The poems that are not destruction—what are they but decay?

III.   Did you read the one about the depression of the poet's brother?
       the one about the bulimia of the poet's daughter?
       the one about the alcoholism of the poet's mother?
       the one about the leukemia of the poet's father?
       the one about the dementia of the poet's grandma?
       the one about the divorce of the poet's sister?
       the one about the autism of the poet's nephew?
       the one about the drowning of the poet's uncle?
       the one about the diabetes of the poet's aunt?
       the one about the disappearance of the poet's neighbor?
       the one about the incarceration of the poet's friend?
       the one about the suicide of the poet?

IV.   We live where it's light, but write where it's dark,
       thrill at the thundercloud, shun the sunshine,
       pine for midnight, worship the ontology of catastrophe.

V.   The poet says, "Somebody's done for."
       The poet says, "You must change your life."
       The poet says, "My mind's not right."
       The poet says, "I weep like a child for the past."
       The poet says, "I must lie down where all the ladders start."
       The poet says, "If I stepped out of my body, I would break."

Bill Yarrow

Not Wanting to Write

I don't want to write about suicide
or surgery, fantasies or accidents,
inheritance or capital gains. I don't want
to write about the body indulged, desires
denied, tortures invented, pleasures innate,
the instinct to wickedness, the pull toward
God. I don't want to write about apathy,
audaciousness, or apostasy. I don't want
to make up specific details of universal
experience or recall the smells of childhood.
I don't want to ransack my imagination
for booty or autopsy society's corpse. I don't
want to crawl into corners, investigate attics,
or poke in holes. I'm done with ambition,
with all the strings and pulleys of art.
I just want to lie down

in the ~~sunrise of your heart~~
in the ~~garden of your heart~~
in the ~~orchard of your heart~~
in the ~~river of your heart~~
in the ~~forest of your heart~~
in the ~~seashore of your heart~~
in the ~~harbor of your heart~~
in the ~~village of your heart~~
in the ~~chapel of your heart~~
in ~~the~~ your heart
~~in~~ your ~~heart~~

What the Hell Am I Doing?

> "Can you make no use of nothing, nuncle?"
>
> —*King Lear*, Act I, sc. iv

My daughter is a therapist. She's started reading my
poems. She's noticed something curious: in each of them
the same thing happens: nothing. In one she tells me
a woman in bad car accident just stares at her hands.
In another a man travels three thousand miles looking
for a key he refuses to use. In another a bald man sits
in a plaid chair and watches a blank screen. There's another
where a boy boards a bus and stares out the window
at darkness. A man standing on a foothill bleeds into his boots.
An atheist gets stung by a bee and watches his hand swell up.
A son returns home to a deranged parent. A college boy
watches his grandmother die. A despairing writer sees
acorns fall from a tree. A man with a blonde mustache
loiters by rusting monkey bars. An exile learns his mother
died in a suspicious fire. A tourist strolls past a hotel
famous because a suicide happened there. Some things
of course do happen, she notices. Someone is slapped.
Someone fakes incontinence. After a beautiful dream,
someone wakes up crying. Someone books a cruise.
Someone gambles at a casino. Someone floats in the sea.
These are alternative nothings, she tells me. "Is that a
technical term?" I ask, wondering what the criterion is
not to be nothing. "You want me to write about something?
Is that it?" *No, not necessarily. But I don't like to see you
write about nothing.* "Why? Johnson said you need something
to fill up the vacuity of life." *And you choose nothing with which
to fill life's empty bucket?* "Well maybe nothing just picked me."
I find you curious, Dad. "That's not something either, Sweetie."

Bill Yarrow

PURVEYORS OF LEECHES

I.

In "Resolution and Independence"
Wordsworth admired the firm mind
of the old leech gatherer on the moor.

To me, he's the emblem of the writer
walking into the scummy pond of life
waiting for the vile leeches of heartache,
the stinging leeches of heartbreak,
the slimy leeches of broken hope
to attach themselves, like dust to a
mirror, to his torso, legs, and arms.

At home, he'll pick the sticky pieces
off him and put them in a water jug
to sell to all those suppurating souls
desperate for relief from bleakness
of spirit, or illness of body, or torpor
of mind. "Who'll buy my leeches?"
cries the poet with several squirming
in his hand. "Who'll buy my leeches?"
cries the novelist, bending under
the weight of hundreds in a sack.

"Leeches for sale! Leeches for sale!"

II.

I am a purveyor of leeches. All my
friends are purveyors of leeches.
We meet weekly to compare our wares.
She buys my leeches, and I buy his leeches,
and he buys her leeches, and we attach
them to each other, and they suck out
all the vileness of living alone, of living

Blasphemer

in groups, of living in pairs, in short,
of living, and, for a while, we are healthy
and happy until someone comes along
and explodes our hopes or extinguishes our
hearts and then we ache and bleat for sticky
leeches, for where else can succor be found?

Dislocutions

My boyfriend lives in Attica

The wedding colors will be ochre, black, anisette, and beige

Politically, the coalition failed due to a lack of application of confluence

Leonard sat in the shaded corner of the deck

The opposite of "lui," she explained, is "elle"

It's futile. Can't you see it's futile?

I shall season your petition with gravity

Come, I will show you the way to Hillcrest

Not I! Not I! Not I! Not I! Not I!

To a cinematographer, color is a drug (Jean Juan)

You've never read Klopstock?

If you want me, I'll be on the lanai

Unaccommodated woman; overaccommodated man

Artichokes with ginger, cube steak with fennel, potatoes with nutmeg

The cymbal concert will be Tuesday in the Taj Mahal of Ontario

A sentence which reserves its inventive zest for the end is called periodic

My favorite writer? Quintilian

She wanted to put the "o man!" back in romance

A letter written from the bottom up would end with the salutation

I went to Japan and all I got was this lousy tanka

Assonance in "Ulysses"

Bellicose boys. Jericho noise. Varicose veins

Shakespeare, Cowper, Blake, Wordsworth, Yeats: all Williams

Q: This name in Basque means "owns a new house." A: What is "Xavier"?

A Perfect Day for Banana or The Bride Comes to Yellow

I need to reread The Prisoner of Zenda

ANTHROPOMETAMORPHISM

I have known a head become
a callus, matriculate, stop
shaving, move to Vegas

I have known a mouth become
a gland, install a flange,
sail to the Western Isles

I have known a bicep become
a pustule, argue its authority,
sabotage the badinage

I have known a skin tag become
a tear duct, take up the flugelhorn,
extrapolate the Florentines

I have known a heart become
a kidney, vibrate, grow
wings, fly off into the piss

Bill Yarrow

Charlatan Art

I bought some charlatan art
and hung it on the wall.

My friends applauded my savvy,
my relatives my excellent taste.

Then I won an iPad from the credit union.
The next day I got a merit raise at work.

Well, I bought another charlatan piece
and that night my wife re-decided to love me.

Soon after, all my kids moved back to Illinois.
Oyez! There is tall magic in chicanery.

When the Blackhawks made the playoffs and my lupus disappeared,
I went back to the charlatan well.

Lo and behold, Pluto was renamed a planet,
Tolstoy was awarded a posthumous Nobel.

FOEHN CALL

The Foehn wind "is a type of dry, warm, down-slope wind that occurs in the lee (downwind side) of a mountain range." (Wikipedia). It is "notorious for causing bizarre human behavior. Suicides, domestic violence, depression, and nausea have all been attributed to the Swiss foehn" (*Seed Magazine*, December 21, 2009)

for Marc K.

I was looking at getting a Christopher Smart phone
but the price was just insane.

There's a new Sylvia Plath phone on the market
but it only comes in black.

When my Plath phone stopped working, I traded it in
for an Anne Sexton. What was I thinking?

I am considering buying a Joyce Carol Oates phone
but do I really have that much to say?

My friend lent me his porno phone, but it's a nightmare.
Once you turn it on, it won't stop fucking with you.

After all that, I decided on a Jesus phone.
How can you go wrong with a battery that's everlasting?

Bill Yarrow

MODERN LOVE

I.

He held her	tight.
He kissed her	hard.
He loved her	good.
He turned her	on.
She wanted him	bad.
She treated him	nice.
She moved him	in.
She made him	beg.

II.

He got her	tight.
She got him	high.
He smacked her	butt.
She liked it	rough.
He fucked her	up.
She fucked him	over.
He turned her	in.
She told him	off.
He called her	bluff.
She tossed him	out.

III.

She wanted him	near.
He held her	close.
She fucked him	up and down.
He fucked her	over and over.
She loved him	silly.
He made her	purr.

She asked him   to.
He told her   no.

She turned him   away.
He pushed her   aside.

Part Three:

To Pluck Out the Heart of My Blasphemy

FROM JACK SPICER'S LETTER TO LORCA

I would like to make poems out of real objects

the lemon
to be a lemon
that the reader
could cut
          or squeeze
          or taste
a real lemon
               like a newspaper in a collage
               is a real newspaper

I would like the moon in my poems to be a real moon

one which could be
            suddenly

covered
             with a cloud
             that has nothing
             to do
with the poem
             a moon utterly
independent of images

The imagination pictures the real

I would like
to point to the real
disclose it

to make a poem
that has no sound in it

but the pointing of a finger

BOSCH'S LAST WORDS

I.

Now
leave
me

I
go
my

way
alone
I

must
go
out

for
I
have

work
in
hand

and
insects
waiting

for
me
to

talk

                                                               busi-
                                                               ness

                              II.

                              Now, leave
                              me. I

                              go my
                              way alone.

                              I must
                              go out

                              for I
                              have work

                              in hand
                              and insects

                              waiting for
                              me to

                              talk
                              business.

III.

Now,
LEAVE me.
I go my way

ALONE.
I must go

Bill Yarrow

out

for I have
WORK
in hand and insects

waiting
for me to talk
BUSINESS.

Dadd's Imagination

I.

Dadd was, by force of circumstance,
an artist who lived outside the art community.

II.

He was a young man
when he killed his father.

III.

He spent the rest of his life
in confinement in Bethlem hospital

where he produced a series of paintings
on the subject of fairies.

IV.

The most elaborate of these is
"The Fairy Feller's Master Stroke."

V.

It is a painstakingly detailed work.

VI.

It depicts a crowd of little people
standing among towering daisies

and watching a scene whose import must forever
remain locked in Dadd's imagination.

A poem comprised of lines from *The Symbolists* by Michael Gibson. Harry N. Abrams, 1988. p. 70.

Bill Yarrow

COLERIDGE ON URINE

What a beautiful Thing
Urine is,
in a Pot,
brown, yellow,
transpicuous, the Image,
diamond shaped
of the Candle in it,
especially, as
it now appeared,
I having emptied the Snuffers
into it & the Snuff
floating about, &
painting all-shaped Shadows
on the Bottom.

Coleridge *Notebook* I, #1766.

I Wonder About the Trees

I stole forth dimly in the dripping pause.
I let myself in at the kitchen door.
I slumbered with your poems upon my breast.

I found a dimpled spider, fat and white.
I went to the physician to complain.
I farm a pasture where the boulders lie.

I love to toy with the Platonic notion.
I would build my house of crystal.
I never happened to contrast.

I walked down alone Sunday after church.
I turned to speak to God.
I didn't like the way he went away.

I felt the chill of the meadow underfoot.
I didn't make you know how glad I was.
I dwell in a lonely house I know.

I advocate a semi-revolution.
I never dared be radical when young.
I stayed the night for shelter at a farm.

I have wished the bird to fly away.
I often see flowers from a passing car.
I wonder about the trees.

A poem of first lines beginning with "I" from Robert Frost poems.

Bill Yarrow

Found Poem

On an exceptionally hot evening
early in June, a young man
came out of the garret

in which he lived in S. Place
and walked slowly as if in hesitation
towards K. Bridge

The waters rose
on the earth
one hundred and fifty days

I concluded that I might take as a general rule
the principle that all the things which we very clearly and distinctly conceive
are true

This poem stitches together sentences from Dostoyevsky's *Crime and Punishment*, Genesis, and Descartes' "Essay on Method."

SOMETHING MAX BECKMANN SAID

the
stronger
and
more
profound
my
determination
grows

to
grasp
the
unutterable
things of
this
world

the
tighter
I
keep
my
mouth
shut

and
the
harder
I
try
to
capture

the
terrible

Bill Yarrow

thrilling
monster
of
life's
vitality

Max Beckmann in Miesel's *Voices of German Expressionism.*

Blasphemer

THE WATER

At every step we took inland
the conviction forced itself upon us
that we were in a country
differing essentially from any
hitherto visited by civilized men.

We saw nothing
with which we had been
formerly conversant.

The trees resembled no growth of either the torrid
the temperate or the northern frigid zones
and were altogether unlike those of the lower southern latitudes
we had already traversed.

The very rocks were novel in their mass
their color and their stratification

and the streams themselves
utterly incredible as it may appear
had so little in common
with those of other climates

that we were scrupulous of tasting them
and indeed
had difficulty in bringing ourselves to believe
that their qualities were purely those of nature.

At a small brook which crossed our path
(the first we had reached)
Too-wit and his attendants halted to drink.

On account of the singular character of the water
we refused to taste it
supposing it to be polluted

Bill Yarrow

and it was not until some time afterward
we came to understand
that such was the appearance of the streams
throughout the whole group.

I am at a loss to give a distinct idea
of the nature of this liquid
and cannot do so
without many words.

Although it flowed with rapidity in all declivities
where common water would do so
yet never except when falling in a cascade
had it the customary appearance of limpidity.

It was nevertheless in point of fact
as perfectly limpid as any limestone water in existence
the difference being only in appearance.

At first sight
and especially in cases where little declivity was found
it bore resemblance as regards consistency
to a thick infusion of gum arabic in common water.

But this was only the least remarkable
of its extraordinary qualities.

It was not colorless
nor was it of any one uniform color—
presenting to the eye as it flowed
every possible shade of purple
like the hues of a changeable silk.
This variation in shade
was produced in a manner
which excited as profound astonishment
in the minds of our party

as the mirror had done in the case of Too-wit.

Upon collecting a basinful
and allowing it to settle thoroughly
we perceived that:

- the whole mass of liquid
    was made up of a number of distinct veins
    each of a distinct hue
- that these veins did not commingle
- and that their cohesion was perfect
    in regard to their own particles among themselves
    and imperfect in regard to neighboring veins

Upon passing the blade of a knife
athwart the veins
the water closed over it immediately
as with us
and also in withdrawing it
all traces of the passage of the knife
were instantly obliterated.

If however the blade
was passed down accurately
between the two veins
a perfect separation was effected
which the power of cohesion
did not immediately rectify.

The phenomena of this water
formed the first definite link
in that vast chain of apparent miracles
with which I was destined
to be at length encircled.

Found poem. From *The Narrative of Arthur Gordon Pym* by Edgar Allan Poe. Chapter 18.

Bill Yarrow

The Kraft-Ebing Poems

Case #106

when she was about ten years old
   she thought that her mother no longer loved her

so she put matches in her coffee
   to make herself sick

that she might thus excite
   her mother's affection for her

Case #88

on account of his impotence
   the patient applied to Dr. Hammond

who treated his epilepsy
   with bromides

and advised him
   to hang a boot over his bed

imagine his wife to be a shoe
   and to look at it fixedly during intercourse

Case #8

   as a child he was not affectionate
and was cold toward his parents

   as a student he was peculiar
and retiring, preoccupied with self

   he was well endowed mentally and given to much reading
but eccentric after puberty

   alternating between religious enthusiasm
and materialism

Blasphemer

now studying theology
now natural sciences

at the university his fellow students
took him for a fool

for he read Jean Paul
almost exclusively

Case #89
on his marriage night
  he remained cold

until he brought to his aid
  a picture

of an ugly woman's head wearing a night cap
  whereupon coitus was immediately successful

Case #36
  she must stand at the window
awaiting him with her face done up

  and on his entrance into the room
complain of severe toothache

  he is sorry for her
asks particularly about the pain

  takes the cloth off
and puts it on again

  he never touches her
yet finds complete sexual satisfaction in this act

Bill Yarrow

Case #55

on their wedding night
    he forced a towel and soap into her hands

and without any other expression of love
    asked her to lather his chin and neck as if for shaving

the inexperienced young wife did it
    and during the first weeks of married life

was not a little astonished to learn
    the secrets of marital intimacy in this way alone

Case #102

    the patient in a circle of erotic ideas
grows more and more peculiar

    he avoids the society
of women

    associates with them
only for the sake of music

    and only when two witnesses
are with him

Case #83

his dreams are filled
    with aprons

Blasphemer

CHRISTIAN MORALS CENTO

1. Annihilate not the Mercies of God by the Oblivion of Ingratitude
2. Punish not thyself with Pleasure
3. Be not a *Hercules furens* abroad, and a Poltroon within thyself
4. If Avarice be thy Vice, yet make it not thy Punishment
5. Owe not thy Humility unto humiliation from adversity
6. Make not the consequence of Virtue the ends thereof
7. Love is not to be made by magnifying Glasses
8. *Cato* is much to be pitied who mangled himself with poniards

from "Christian Morals" by Sir Thomas Browne.

Bill Yarrow

Helix Poem

Sorrow
gazing up
is a kind
into the blackness
of rust
I saw myself
of the soul
as a creature
which
driven and derided
every new idea
by vanity
contributes
and my eyes burned
in its passage
with anguish
to scour
and anger
away

A braid poem made of the penultimate sentence of *Rambler* No. 47 by Samuel Johnson and the concluding sentence of "Araby" by James Joyce.

Blasphemer

Resolution at Midnight

I.

There was a roaring unhelped by any wind.
The owlet's cry is rising calm and bright.
The inmates of my cottage voice abstruser musings.
At my side the air is filled with pleasant noise.

'Tis calm, so calm, that it disturbs the morning's birth:
sea, hill, and wood running races
with all the numberless goings-on of life
raises a mist that lies and quivers not.

I was a Traveller then, the sole unquiet thing.
I heard the woods and distant waters roar dim sympathies.
The pleasant season did my heart employ the idling spirit
and all the ways of men, so vain.

Echo or mirror of joys!
How oft in our dejection do we sink to watch
fears and fancies of sky-lark warbling in the sky.

From morn to evening, all the hot fair day,
such a happy child of earth am I.

With a wild pleasure, falling on mine ear
and from all care so gazed I
till the soothing things I dreamt:
solitude, pain of heart, distress, and poverty.

And so I brooded all the following morn
as if life's business were a summer mood
fixed with mock study still rich.

A hasty glance, and still my heart leaped up.

Bill Yarrow

Build for him! Sow for him! And at his call
townsman, or aunt, or sister more beloved!

I thought of Chatterton that sleepest,
who fill up the interspersèd vacancies
by spirits so beautiful it thrills my heart
but thereof come in the end despondency.

And think that thou shalt learn far other lore,
a leading from above, a something given,
in the great city, pent 'mid cloisters dim
when I with these untoward thoughts
shalt wander like a breeze.

I saw a Man before me unawares
of ancient mountain and beneath the clouds.

As a huge stone is sometimes seen to lie
and mountain crags, so shalt thou see and hear
wonder to all who do the same espy
of that eternal language which thy God
endued with sense: Himself in all,
and all things in Himself of rock or sand reposeth.

Make it ask whether the summer clothe the general earth
feet and head betwixt the tufts of snow on the bare branch
as if some dire constraint of pain or rage
smokes in the sun-thaw, whether the eave-drops fall
a more than human weight upon his frame.

Or if the secret ministry
of frost upon a long grey staff
of shaven wood to the quiet moon.

Blasphemer

II.

The frost motionless as a cloud
loud as before and moveth all together
left me to that solitude, which fixedly did look peacefully
as if he had been reading in a book with its strange side,
to him did say, "This populous village."

A gentle answer did the old Man make
(inaudible as dreams!) and him with
further words which fluttered on the grate,
"This is a lonesome place. Methinks its motion
in this hush of nature broke from the sable orbs
of his yet-vivid eyes, making it a companionable form,"
but each in solemn order followed each by its own moods,
choice word and measured phrase
above the reach of thought in Scotland.

I gazed upon the bars that to these waters he had come
with unclosed lids—hazardous and wearisome—
whose bells roamed from moor to moor
like articulate sounds of things to come
and in this way he gained an honest maintenance.

Sleep prolonged my dreams but now his voice to me
was like a stream. Mine eye and the whole body
of the Man did seem if the door half opened
or like a man from some far region sent
for still I hoped to see the *stranger's* face,

My former thoughts returned: the fear that kills
my play when we were clothed alike!
Cold, pain, and labor, and all fleshly ills,
whose gentle breathings, heard in this deep calm,
perplexed, and longing to be comforted, pauses:
"How is it that you live?"

Bill Yarrow

With tender gladness, far and wide
and in far other scenes the waters of the pools.
saw naught but they have dwindled long
by slow decay by lakes and sandy shores.

While he was talking thus, the lonely place
which image in their bulk both lakes and shores
in my mind's eye I seemed to see him,
lovely and intelligible, wandering about alone and silently,
who from eternity doth teach the same discourse renewed.

Great universal Teacher!
(He shall mold with demeanor kind to thee.)

I could
have
laughed
myself
to greenness.

"God," said I.

while the nigh thatch heard only,
"Hang them up in icicles."

A lyrical braid. An alternation of lines and phrases from William Wordsworth's "Resolution and Independence"
and Samuel Taylor Coleridge's "Frost at Midnight."

Blasphemer

THREE STANZAS ENDING WITH A LINE FROM R. CRUMB

The tin roofs of the blue banks have been pockmarked by hail.
The squirrels will not stop peeing on the trees.
I'm still alive in the flatlands of Dixon.

The raw cost of loss.
The past recuses the sutures of the future.
I'm still alive in the flatlands of Dixon.

The fallow ballot has been cast.
I saw a film composed entirely of jump cuts.
I'm still alive in the flatlands of Dixon.

"I'm still alive in the flatlands of Dixon" comes from an autobiographical entry in R. *Crumb Sketchbook,* by Robert Crumb. Volume 10 (*June 1975 – Feb. 1977*). Seattle: Fantagraphics Books, 2004. NP.

Bill Yarrow

Part Four:

This Above All: To Thine Own Self, Be Blasphemous

Kicking out the Enjambs

Another day, another dolor. I
can be iambic when I want to be!
For heaven's sake, the forgotten man has
been forsaken! The forsaken man for
gotten! For heaven's forsaken! Looky,
everything's *très* mystique. Usury for
you? Misery for me. Agita for
breakfast? Telos for dinner. What price, tag?
Wake me when the narcoleptics arrive.

Don't Touch That Bare Wire He Said Dialectically

My wife wants to go out for dinner.
Hogan's Gyros? Sure, why not?

In the parking lot I see someone
has dropped a book: Groddeck's

The It Ching. I'm tempted to pick it up
but, afraid of contagion, I let it lie.

Today is The Festival of Abstinence:
holiday of holidays! Before us the Dusk

Queen bows. In the steep grease
of diminished light, ultramarine

appetite seizes the upper hand.
Hadn't I read men are all stomachs

tightening at the thought of
Isabellas? Strange what ideas

flash across a famished mind.
Smiling, I tell my demiurge

about the copy editor sentenced
to the House of Corrections.

And Revisions? she quips.
Haha! Then the conversation

turns serious during which I
reconnoiter Hell and consider

moving to France, land of Moliere
Montaigne Voltaire and Poe.

Bill Yarrow

I was late, I explain, because
I got held up at the bank.

A likely excuse! she sputters.
You were with your hussy!

What if I was? I mean, what
if I were? *What! You admit it?*

No, I admit nothing. Why
should I? I committed nothing.

*You commit nothing, you submit nothing,
you remit nothing!* And you, you <u>permit</u>

nothing! *I'm going; I've lost my appetite.*
What? No longer hungry? Quel surprise!

*

At home, in bed, they ate their words.
Pero mejor comer las palabras que ya han sido tragadas!

THE PISSANT CANTOS

Story One:

In Jan Steen's "The Doctor's Visit" of 1663, the doctor's
feet are odd. They are shaped like the hats of elves.
The doctor wears a pointed cap, bends over and takes
the pulse of a seated woman dressed in an orange gown.
Eyes on the chandelier above her head, she leans back.
A gray scarf bisects her bodice, trails between her legs.
The details of the room include a bed warmer, a wall
lute, and a courtship picture in a tawny frame.

Story Two:

A red bathtub. A nude beach in Big Sur.
Oil painting of me in yellow pants. Hiking
in Appalachia. Camping in Key West. Xmas
in Westchester. Redd Foxx at the Playboy Club.
Black condoms in silk envelopes. Over her bed,
a charcoal portrait of Origen. A ravine transforms
into a beach. The call of gulls. The *sang-froid* of miles.

Story Three:

We crossed into Belgium just after midnight.
The border guards searched the van, unwrapped
the picture you were bringing to your aunt, made
us strip down to our skivvies, even opened
our suppository vials. They were looking for drugs,
but we fooled them; we just had tea.

Story Four:

"You lost the tip of your finger, too?" she
asked him that night at dinner. He held
up his bandaged ring finger and nodded.
"Why are there no guards on those machines?

Bill Yarrow

How many more of us have to lose precious flesh?"

Story Five:

The Blues Project was playing at Town Hall.
I went with Alan and the two Robbies.
Woody's Truck Stop went on first. In the car ride
home, I grew my hair and threw away my shoes.

Story Six:

In conversation, she was like a bear, trapping
her prey between herself and a wall, sinking
her teeth into the soft skin of contradiction.

Story Seven:

A car. A piece of fruit. The interstate. Rain.
Three lanes narrow to one. Rind everywhere.

Story Eight:

He was very very good at Skee-ball as a child.

CENTURIES OF FALLING

I am falling, falling out of my body,
falling like snow into a new volcano.

I am falling, falling out of my body,
falling like midnight onto mice.

I am falling, falling out of my body,
falling like sand into the wet hair of the world.

I am falling, falling out of my body,
falling like raindrops onto tiny sprockets of light.

I am falling, falling out of my body,
falling like sugar into God's hot caffeine.

Bill Yarrow

All Kind of Ruin

They cracked both of Jimmy's shins.
Gambling debt just like in the movies
except in real life it's a little more
tearful, a little less marauding. Aunt
Dot didn't see it. She was diabetes
blind or dead by then. I don't remember.
The main thing is to avoid heartache
but only the frozen know how to do that.
Look! The arteries of time are running out
of blood. Look! The lungs of love are caked
with soot. When your mind is a runic jewel,
you don't need book knowledge. Still, there
is "the algebra of need," the calculus of junk,
the addict's infatuation with a run of raw luck.

END OF SHIFT

He fell back against the pillows
inert as a noble gas. I watched
his body weave in and out of
delirium, listened to it suck all
the sleep out of the tired air.
He was losing his fight with
malaria, but you would never
know it from his dreams
which were fierce and fearless
ruddy and red, in which all the
weapons were drawn, all poised
to clash. He was fighting the
bees, who had the heads of
lobsters and bellowed like
mittens in the microwave.
Against him was the Yakuza
in league with the Mariana
Trench. Italian circus clowns
wearing emerald ties bubbled
up from the pork-pie deep
and made snipping sounds
as they broke the surface of
Migrant Bay. The agricultural fair
was interrupted by an invasion
of piebald workmen with stalks
of corn growing out of their backs.
His body heaved arrhythmically.
Was I watching him die or recover?
I couldn't tell. Ten minutes more
and I was done for the day.
Someone else may witness
the wry dénouement. I will be
miles away where the porous
walls are covered in bituminous
cheese, where the scorpion
clocks are drawing the water
for their velveteen candle baths.

Bill Yarrow

EXCOMMUNICADO

1.

they tied him to a louver
and piled up hickory sticks

the flames gushed through the slats
and then burned down the house

not every punishment proceeds
without a hitch

2.

in walks the ghost with wireless hands
the hacksaw complexion
the jackoff heart

Gabriel in a zebra suit

3.

like a dog's first whiff of cinnamon
integrity is confident
it can annihilate all perfidy

4.

here's what can be glimpsed:

a rose degraded to a thorn
a man etherized on a couch
all the hymns of Hymen sung to the music of crucifixes

5.

the Moon is our conscience
we shall not wane

Etta Kapusta

I met her in the lobby of The Electric Factory where Eddie and I had come to see Ten Years After. It wasn't a lobby exactly. More like a blackened foyer, a dim cavern, a dark tunnel, fashionably dreary, something out The Magic Theater in *Steppenwolf*: "For madmen only." Made me forget the bleakness of Arch Street. She was wearing a yellow sundress and strapless sandals, a style of the time. She looked like Julie Christie. I couldn't stop looking at her. I deliberately bumped up against her and she smiled. We started talking, so I got Eddie to switch seats with her.

"Come see Ferlinghetti with me at the Free Library next week."

When we got there, the place was packed. We were part of the overflow crowd. Foyer experience redux. We heard him read from *A Coney Island of the Mind*, his voice piped in from the main hall. He started with the poem about the symbolic birds sailing through the straits of Demos. I didn't get the allusion to Pound, but she did and I loved that. Here was someone who knew about Pound. About Pavese. About Pinter. About Paton. Someone I could talk to about Kosinski and Kesey and Kazantzakis and Kleist. That's what we all want, isn't it? Someone who will look into our soul without being tempted to toss in a stone.

I held on to this woman. I held on to her as if she were a bus token, a movie ticket, a payroll check, a deposit slip. I held on to her in the Theater of Living Arts, in the Academy of Music, on Roosevelt Boulevard, in 30th Street Station, in the ballroom of the Bellevue-Stratford, but, in a moment of inattention, I relaxed my grip.

She floated off.

Over Coney Island.

Across the Verrazano Narrows.

Through the straits of Demos.

And now, it's ten years after. And ten years after that. And ten plus ten years even after that. And all I have left is a shelf full of books no one wants to read—Kesey,

Paton, Kleist, Pound, Kosinski, Pavese, Kazantzakis, Pinter. But Ferlinghetti. People still read Ferlinghetti. They do. They hold on to Ferlinghetti, *like he was a crucifix*. He was a good poet, he is a good poet, even though he never returned to Philly. I don't hold that against him though. But he should've come back. I wish he would've come back. Come back, Ferlinghetti! Bring her with you! Bring Etta with you!

In My Hometown

in my hometown
pinhead Joe plays mumbly-peg
alone with a sharpened spoon

in my hometown
manila is the flavor
and cul de sac is the address

in my hometown
the Catholic girls know all
the words to "Louie, Louie"

in my hometown
the post office serves
Doritos and lime beer

in my hometown
yellow Ford Falcons
people Old York Road

in my hometown
all the crosses on Mt. Carmel Ave
are upside down

in my hometown
the thalidomide baby
just turned sweet sixteen

Bill Yarrow

MOTHER DIED TOMORROW

nasturtium
epoxy
ulcer
unguent

words she can't define

delinquent
flamingo
invisible
powerboat

words she can't pronounce

death of Uncle Aminadab
anniversary trip to Boulder
birth of Joey
birth of Joey Jr

memories that no longer exist

the golf course fire
the wedding by the lake
the Christmas the car wouldn't start
skylights in the bedroom

memories that no longer make sense

to serene a ballerina
to quickly the stars
to immunize her income tax
to remarry Guadalcanal

her dreams

radish hearts

Sinai nights
a vanished autumn
a burnished cross

her hopes

because
unless
whatever
although

subordinating conjunctions she mistakes for nouns

Bill Yarrow

Here Comes the Sun

She lies on her stomach by the side of the pool staring into her towel. On her back, I can make out a pastel isthmus, surgery's pink art or charlatan's scab, I can't tell which. She is beautiful as rare roast beef is beautiful. I stare at the curve of her calf, a crescent of red flesh. I recognize her from the oncologist's office, her appointment had directly preceded mine, but who am I to cast blame? I am in the water myself, a little cool today but tomorrow sure to be hot or hotter. What tomorrow is not hotter than today? I pull myself out and look for some shade, but there is none to be had. Maybe sunscreen will protect me. If not sunscreen, then Athena.

I throw on my shirt and cover my legs as best I can. The sun's the enemy. Was that always the case? Or was I just too stupid to notice? I'm not a good judge of character. I've made friends with pestilence and shiftlessness, hypocrites with swords. I've shaken hands with traitors. The baleful will inherit the earth. Unless the sun gets them first. Praise the Lord.

I should (shouldn't I?) try to save that woman. Why? Because no good deed 'scapes whipping. But she looks the kind that detests salvation. One of those who no doubt resents amelioration too. Well, salvation's not everyone's bag. How sad though to see her incinerate by degrees. I'll alert her she's burning. (Aren't we all?) We're all sinners. Me for sure.

I jump back in the water and wade. But just before I submerge my head, I turn back for another glimpse of her. She is beautiful, well worth frying for, her lissome frame mistress of every billboard in every shade of red, her lithe corpus consort of every flag carved of ruddy color. Long may she wave, I wish her that, even as I see and grieve her intrinsic softness abraded by full-frontal doom.

Paris in the the Spring

he thought of her
urgently as one might
recall the occasion
of a prayer

she thought of him
absently as one might
recall the color
of a bus

he thought of her
excitedly as one might
recall the orange
of a bird

she thought of him
painfully as one might
recall the stiffness
of a joint

he thought of her
longingly as one might
recall the kindness
of a bed

she thought of him
fearfully as one might
recall the onset
of a storm

Bill Yarrow

Receding Haiku

love weaves a perforated web
between the spikes
of longing

testy liquor goes to bed
next to a nest
of wasps

God in his infinite wisdom
rescinds the free will
of dogs

Part Five:

Get Thee to a Blasphemer

Liz @ Phil

Lil didn't steal his heart
she embezzled it

one of a number of larcenies
Phil endured and forgave

ever since he met her
when he was nineteen

and she was twenty-two
but in a bikini top

and pink pedal pushers
she looked sixteen

so he walked taller than he was and she
pretended the hair on his lip was manly

love was an acid that etched
their hope into a metal present

but before ten years had passed
their loneliness had hardened

into indifferent sticky rapture
and permanent part-time jobs

abortions, bad bosses, half-hearted
infidelities, bankruptcy...

time felt like a kitten
wrapped in a rattlesnake

but implacable happiness
was also on its way

FIFTY YEARS STUPID

Missy, you write to me that fifty years
ago I broke your heart and in all that time
it hasn't healed. Really? Hasn't healed?
Come on! But I do believe you when you
say I broke your heart. I'm sure I did.
I was a selfish prick. I did a lot of stupid
things when I was brash and fourteen
and didn't know anything about anything.
Forgive me. I didn't mean to cause you
pain. For me, fourteen was the beginning
of a decade of confusion, resulting in an
early marriage and instant family when
my wife (of forty years) had quadruplets
when she was twenty. Broken hearts? Who
hasn't had at least one? But who hasn't
recovered? A broken heart is the deepest
of wounds, but subsequent love is the balm
that initiates the scab. I'm right, you know.

You'd like to get together. Really? What for?
I would only if I were a character in a novel
by Alice Munro or Julian Barnes, but I'm not
so forget it. No can do. OK? Look, I feel
badly (or is it bad?) that I broke your heart.
These things happen. They happen to a lot
of people. That even happened to my kids.
Four broken hearts in one year! What an
orgy of attempted consolation that was!
There was so much wetness in the house
from constant crying, the walls developed
mold. But back to you. Missy, I don't know
you now, but I remember you as a lovely
person. A beautiful soul. You know why
you're unhappy? Because you refuse to release
the ghosts of your youth. Stop living in the past.
Appreciate what you've got going for you now.
Forget what never almost happened. Kiss life.

Bill Yarrow

On the Point of Understanding

A rusted sword stood
in your chest, the handle
planted in your heart. And just
beneath your paper skin, the jagged
edges of a broken blade. You moaned,
"Please! Grab it! Pull it out!" But how long
was it before you would never ask me again?
I prayed for that sword to grow so I could forge
a better grip. How I watched it grow as the tumor
rose up out of you, an enormous thorn out of a tiny
vine. I wanted to grab it with my nails and yank it free.
Vain hope which wrestled with the fat wrath of sanity. Jesus,
I wanted to do something! But I just sat beside you, staring hard
into darkness and feeling that maybe writing could exorcise a damage
that, I learned, could not help but become the pain of vain remembering.

JULIA

One day she took a lover, a Québécois
mortician, who mollified her spirit as he
mortified her flesh. She found her escape
in a letter from her sclerotic brother whose
neurosis demanded companionship. She'd
fly to Escondido to be his renewal. On her
way to the airport, her cab was rear ended
by a bus. She suffered three broken bones.

Six months later, she was teaching theology
to refugees from EST. Her brother was in rehab,
his prognosis good. She felt healthy and happy,
no clouds anywhere. Pseudocyesis does that.

Bill Yarrow

MAÎTRE DAVE

He asked me to bury him in Reno
but cremation in Trenton was more his style.

I did do one thing he requested: I nailed his dog
tags to the alder tree outside the Frontier Hotel.

The last time I saw him was in an assisted-
living facility in Pennsauken.

                              He stuck out
a wine-dark tongue and punched me
in the chest.

                Poor one-eyed Uncle Dave—
blinded when a fruit fly flew into his eye

nonplussed when two hitchhikers sitting
in his backseat smacked his balding head
with a ball-peen hammer and stole his car.

He had a mind like a whorehouse martini
and a tumor the size of Newark in his gut.

During WWII, he joined the Marines
because he thought the uniforms looked cool.

He Spreadeth Sharp Pointed Things Upon the Mire

My uncle looks into the bleached eye of his cat and asks
    "What happened to my ear?"
The meerkat's eye replies:
    "You had cancer. Remember?
They had to cut off your ear to save you."

My uncle looks into the smudged window of his oven and asks
    "What happened to Maude?"
The sundered oven replies:
    "She had cancer. Remember?
They had to cut her out of your body to save you."

My uncle looks into the blistered photo montage and asks
    "Where's Colin? He'll be late for the swim meet."
The designer frame replies:
    "He had cancer. Remember?
They had to cut him out of your hopes to save you."

My uncle looks into his aluminum shaving mirror and says
    "Why did they want to save me? I didn't want to be saved."
The dented mirror replies:
    "Who clothed the horse's neck with thunder?
Who can discover the garment of his face?"

Bill Yarrow

PICKING THE BARK OFF EXPERIENCE

As he gets into the oil-soaked tub,
he recognizes the Jupiter Symphony
playing on the floor below.

Any minute now, the waiter will
bring him his lobster omelet.

After breakfast, he dresses and heads
for the blackjack tables. When he
wins a million dollars, he will stop.

He remembers his mother's dead body,
the reunion strippers at the funeral.

Carrying a mimosa in a fluted glass,
he fights my way through the lobby
packed with firefighters from Marietta.

His mind is full of anchors and Bar Harbor.

Nothing Beside Remains

It was the early 80s. My students carried
guns. My colleagues died of AIDS.
My bachelor neighbor was a cineaste.
I walked the rent-controlled boulevards
of Sunnyside and watched the glib sun
set over loquacious Manhattan. Every day's
evaporated apogee had its inky epitaph.
We exist only insofar as we are remembered.
The time we went to Carroll Gardens for fake
IDs. Spending New Year's Eve in LeFrak City.
Buying hot coconut kishke from Zabar's.
Dreaming of the Ely Avenue Cleaver.
Under the bridges of Kew Gardens Hills
the invented truth still has street value.

Bill Yarrow

The Scales of Justice

Lobster: You had your opportunity; you had your chance.

Man: Yes, I ought to have done better.

Lobster: You were given instructions; you knew what you had to do.

Man: Yes, I knew; I just couldn't do it.

Lobster: Then you accept your sentence?

Man: How can I not? I wrote it.

Lobster: You are sentenced to tentacles.

Man: The ties that bind...

Lobster: You are condemned to be flailed by fins.

Man: Cutting I deserve.

Lobster: You have been enrolled in Introduction to Gullets.

Man: Of course, I was a devourer.

Lobster: You will come back as an eel.

Man: A life of condign slime.

Lobster: Is there anything you wish to say?

Man: I still don't get what you mean by, "Character is bait."

The Claw Machine

If you stand on the boardwalk and face east
you are looking into the Atlantic Ocean. If you
turn south, you can see the boulders of the jetty
and the sharp silhouettes of the flounder fishermen.
To the north is the amusement pier, Walkerson Fries
Atlantic Taffy, the Friendly Gift Shop, Louie Chop Suey
and the water-balloon game. To the west you stare directly
into my childhood: a penny arcade with showcases of cheap
gifts, rows of Pokerino tables, Skee-Ball lanes, pinball machines.

My mother sits behind the wooden cashier's booth watching
customers plop quarters into a coffin-shaped game with glass
sides and a moving crane. They hunch over the button waiting
for the magic moment to make the three jaws stop, drop, and lock
around a gift. A mustached trucker wants pink foam dice for his girl.
A tourist in short sleeves wants to win his bride a beaded pink watch.
The fourteen-year olds have their slippery eyes on tubes of silver dollars.

There are days the game breaks down. On those days my dad in chinos
and a white undershirt crawls deep inside the claw machine and begins to
monkey with the rotors. My mechanical father, razor blade between his teeth
Allen wrench in his hand, tumor in his chest, glasses on his head, ink-black
hair combed back like sleek Tyrone Power pretending to be canny Stan Carlisle.

Bill Yarrow

Tight Rope

It's hard to say. One minute I was
watching florid waiters carrying
whiskey sours to tourists in striped
tents. The next minute, the pink bay was
littered with corpses. I even saw
a dead monkey. The tsunami rushed
in as *in ev i ta bly* as the
immediate *un rav el ing* of
a marriage you always suspected
was sound. I was lucky to survive.
But we, we who have not yet perished,
we owe our distinction to luck, n'est-ce pas?
Or do you still believe in grace? Or
fate? Or will? Hell, I don't know what I
believe in. The wind, perhaps. Why not?
Wind, blow me to the Galápagos.
I am in need of ancient slowness.

PINK

Among the cherry trees, they fell in love.
Later that month, he took her out for
pink soup and pale pink tea. Together
they peeled and fed each other pink fruit,
ordered expensive pink beef, went on
vacations and viewed pink sunsets
on paradise beaches. His memories
included pink medicine, pink taffy, pink
panties, pink lips. Hers included pink
bubbles, pink slippers, pink horses and
pink sheets. Neither could imagine a heaven
untinged with pink. They were right:
the afterworld is splendiferously pink,
the exact color of a child's new wound.

Bill Yarrow

Departure: Arrival: Return

I.

I am leaving my body: to science,
for a while, for another woman.
I am leaving on a jet plane.

I am leaving in the morning. I am
leaving for parts unknown. I am
leaving but the fighter still remains.

I am taking off on my own, in my
own way, leaving the door unlocked
leaving the dog in the car.

I am leaving for Las Vegas.
I am leaving Las Vegas. I am
leaving for pastures new.

II.

I have arrived. Will you look at
this place! The clouds are
leaning on the sky like winos
against the Thalia. The birds
dot the bare trees like ringworm
on a cow. The sun is resting
on the hill like the final drop
of Thomas Hardy's blood.

III.

I have come back and my bones
are delighted to see me. I encircle
the bakery. I embrace my barber.
I endorse my bank. I am so
happy to walk these wizened

streets, to sup from the civic
trough, to race my horse again
around the calcified church.
Put down your bazooka, Marianne.
Like rusting sumac to the staghorn
aphid, I've come serenely home.

Part Six:

The Rest is Blasphemy

Postscript to a Letter by Flaubert

O, may I be suffused with all the energies of nature
    I have inhaled
        and may they breathe forth
           in my book!

        Powers of artistic emotion, come to my aid!
          Help me resurrect the past!
           Beauty must guide my pen,
             but all must be living and true!

              Have pity on my purpose,
              O God of all souls!
              Give me Strength
              —and Hope!

The Letters of Gustave Flaubert. Volume One. Belknap Press. trans. Francis Steegmuller. Midnight, Saturday-Sunday, June 12-13, 1858.

Erasing Traherne

1. An empty soul is capable of all things.

2. We love the loadstone of desire.

3. I open my mouth that the interior may appear.

4. I will lead you into paths where appear angels.

5. Contemplation is the method of fruition.

6. True love and virtue contemn the world.

7. Confusions give leave.

8. What is in this well of habit?

9. Mind is difficult to retain.

10. To have is the end of desire.

11. The world and I rejoice.

12. All things were made to be created.

13. We are the things of darkness.

14. When things are in their proper places, the earth itself is gold.

15. Alone. Alone. Alone.

16. Your inclinations manifest rich ignorance.

17. To know God is to know terror.

18. The world is a happy loss.

19. You never know yourself till you know the dust.

Bill Yarrow

20. The laws of God are magnified among angels.

21. For there is a disease in him who can never be happy.

22. The stars are no more than so many tennis-balls.

23. Men are marvelously irrational.

24. Is it not a sweet thing to have all ambition removed?

25. The world can take too much joy in reason.

26. Things of the mind, nourished of moisture, feast upon an empty husk.

27. I take pleasure in benefits infinite and eternal.

28. Enjoyment is never delight.

29. You perceive yourself to be the sole heir of the world.

30. Your private estate was the palace of your glory.

31. There is much damned folly in the world.

32. Can any invent ways to make tinseled riches?

33. Truth is able to turn one's stomach.

34. Jewels, resplendent like the stars, transparent like the air, pellucid like the sea, are nothing.

35. Works of joy delight the world.

36. All the foundations of the world are seducing Eden.

37. We need to be ravished that all regions should be full of joys.

38. The height of God's perfection: He implanted in your nature a worm.

39. Honey and honeycomb command you to be glorious.

40. Socrates, being heathen, knew joy.

41. Were there no needs, gods might be satisfied.

42. Infinite want wanted companions.

43. I must lead you into felicity.

44. Empty wants cloy.

45. Wants enjoy joys.

46. Be sensible of what you extinguished or you shall be a hell.

47. To have blessings is to be irrational.

48. No misery is greater than to see all the earth as the world.

49. Is not he most miserable that is most asleep?

50. Upon earth, we learn nothing but hell.

51. Treasures are the ligatures between our wants and love.

52. Love is necessity.

53. You ought to see.

54. He is desolate before universities.

55. The contemplation of the present age is deluge.

56. The elixir of this world is the idle contemplation of man.

57. Eagles are drawn by the scent of commodity.

58. The abyss of desires: the place of happiness.

59. If love be a malefactor, eternity is the spectacle wherein all things appear sprinkled in blood.

60. Saints set on fire illuminateth the world.

61. Contempt is requisite for all things in heaven.

62. What shall I render thee? Perfect wrath, all sharpness, and understanding transient.

63. Ineffable are the misery and happiness of the skull.

64. Orifices covered with filth of beasts and fowls and fishes, all for me.

65. What a confluence of nothing.

66. Is not sight ingratitude?

67. What could I desire, for I am creating an object prone to be sublime?

68. Love loves love.

69. Thou hast given me my desires, infinitely infinite.

70. Desire promoteth heart.

71. There is no defense against necessity.

72. A comprehension insatiable, never fitted for measure.

73. Desire urgeth insufficiency never to decay.

74. Here is a kingdom where all are knit in images.

75. I was deceived by appetite and fell into suffering.

76. At what rate hast thou restored me to my life?

77. I admire sufferings of sinners.

78. Violent glory was created for government.

79. I cannot moderate this particular to knit together honor.

80. The only enjoyment I desire is to delight in a nest of repose.

81. A cold-water deed is a stone.

82. Your companions in fame are like heaps of rubbish.

83. They turn the world into heaven who represent delight.

84. Why be?

85. They despise themselves and do not live.

86. I admire understanding, passion, and tears.

87. O, let me be a mirror.

88. O, let us rend the sun and let the sun be dark.

89. O, dismal spectacle! A mass of miseries and silence: a loving spouse.

90. Most oriently, in most lively colors, appeared our sad estate.

91. To drown the pains of hell, I suffer torments more vehement than love.

92. Nothing is immediately near, nor is it possible to remove it.

93. My body is a chaos, a dark heap of empty faculties.

94. Human will is the whole family, the breadth and length and depth and height.

95. A rushing wind may overflow the means of peace and felicity.

96. I have loved in the near and inward room.

97. Residue delights me.

98. I can never be infinite comfort.

99. We are a peculiar people, zealous of darkness.

100. Things dead seeth their value.

A poem created by erasing sentences, phrases, and words from each of the 100 prose stanzas of "The First Century" of *Centuries of Meditations* by Thomas Traherne.

Hart Crane Pantoum No. 1

O Gorham, I have known moments in eternity.
My satisfactions are far more remote and dangerous than yours.
Life is too scattered for me to savor it any more.
Your figure haunts me like a kind of affectionate caress.

My satisfactions are far more remote and dangerous than yours.
O God that I should have to live within these American restrictions.
Your figure haunts me like a kind of affectionate caress.
Meditation on the sun is all there is.

O God that I should have to live within these American restrictions.
The imagination is the only thing worth a damn.
Meditation on the sun is all there is.
Let us invent an idiom for the proper transposition of jazz into words!

The imagination is the only thing worth a damn.
I pass my goggle-eyed father on the streets.
Let us invent an idiom for the proper transposition of jazz into words!
My writing is hard deciphering.

I pass my goggle-eyed father on the streets.
That funeral was one of the few beautiful things that have happened to me in
Cleveland.
My writing is hard deciphering.
O if you knew how much I am learning!

That funeral was one of the few beautiful things that have happened to me in
Cleveland.
One must be drenched in words.
O if you knew how much I am learning!
Let's write occasionally and be as metropolitan as possible.

One must be drenched in words.

Life is too scattered for me to savor it any more.

Let's write occasionally and be as metropolitan as possible.

O Gorham, I have known moments in eternity.

A pantoum made from lines from *The Letters of Hart Crane 1916-1932*, edited by Brom Weber, University of California Press, Berkeley and Los Angeles, 1965. Out of copyright. Internet Archive.

D.H. Lawrence Ghazal

How many shadows in your soul? Close your eyes, my love, let me
make you blind as the wings of a drenched, drowned bee.

The street lamps in the darkness have suddenly started to bleed.
The hoar-frost crumbles in the sun like the wings of a drenched, drowned bee.

The sick grapes on the chair by the bed, the silk obscure leaves...
Taste, oh taste, and let me taste the wings of a drenched, drowned bee.

A wet bird walks on the lawn like a needle steadfastly. See
the laburnum shimmering like the wings of a drenched, drowned bee.

I who am substance of shadow, I all compact, I own that some of me
is dead tonight as the wings of a drenched, drowned bee.

My beautiful, lonely body, tired and unsatisfied—I wish I bore it more patiently
as dolphins that leap from the sea, as the wings of a drenched, drowned bee.

She bade me follow to her garden where Death has delivered us utterly
full of disappointment and of rain as the wings of a drenched, drowned bee.

Further down the valley the clustered tombstones recede.
My soul lies helpless as the wings of a drenched, drowned bee.

The thought of the lipless voice of the Father shakes me with filigree
and uncanny cold like the wings of a drenched, drowned bee.

The Angel of Judgment has departed again to the Nearness, but surely
my soul's best dream is still the wings of a drenched, drowned bee.

Bill Yarrow

You are strong and passive and beautiful. I will give you all my keys,
you with your face all rich like the wings of a drenched, drowned bee.

A ghazal made from lines in poems from *Amores* by D.H. Lawrence.
SOURCES: • A wet bird walks on the lawn ("A Passing Bell") • As dolphins that leap from the sea ("The Mystic Blue") • As the wings of a drenched, drowned bee ("A Baby Asleep after Pain") • But surely my soul's best dream is still ("Excursion") • Close your eyes, my love, let me make you blind ("A Spiritual Woman") • Death has delivered us utterly ("Brother and Sister") • Full of disappointment and of rain ("Ballad of Another Ophelia") • Further down the valley the clustered tombstones recede ("At the Window") • How many shadows in your soul? ("In a Boat") • I own that some of me is dead to-night ("The End") • I will give you all my keys ("Tease") • I wish I bore it more patiently ("Study") • I who am substance of shadow, I all compact ("Blue") • Like a needle steadfastly ("Patience") • My beautiful, lonely body tired and unsatisfied ("Virgin Youth") • My soul lies helpless ("The Virgin Mother") • See the laburnum shimmering ("Drunk") • She bade me follow to her garden, where ("Snap-Dragon") • Taste, oh taste and let me taste ("Liaison") • The Angel of Judgment has departed again to the Nearness ("The Punisher") • The hoar-frost crumbles in the sun ("Anxiety") • The sick grapes on the chair by the bed ("Malade") • The silk, obscure leaves ("Mating") • The street lamps in the darkness have suddenly started to bleed ("At the Window") • The thought of the lipless voice of the Father shakes me ("Monologue of a Mother") • With filigree and uncanny cold ("The Bride") • You are strong and passive and beautiful ("Reproach") • You with your face all rich ("Scent of Irises")

THE RUINED FORM

Still pouring forth executive desire,
despondence seized again the fallen gods
while we're in the body that's impossible.
With emulous taste that vulgar deed annoys,
dreaming sloth of pallid hue,
let us dine on beans and bacon.

With taste that annoys the emulous gods,
again let us dine on beans and deed
while we're in the body that's desire.
Pouring forth impossible despondence,
still dreaming bacon of vulgar hue,
the fallen executive seized the pallid sloth.

While we're in the pallid despondence
that's vulgar, sloth seized the deed
and emulous bacon of impossible hue.
Let us dine again on fallen beans,
still bodying forth that dreaming taste
and annoy the executive gods.

Let us, dreaming emulous beans,
taste again impossible desire,
dine on bacon that annoys the executive
pouring forth vulgar sloth
with pallid gods that seized despondence
while we're still in the body of fallen hue.

With vulgar taste, that emulous deed
seized sloth and still desire, while
in the body, despondence, the pallid
executive, pouring forth on beans and fallen
bacon, dreaming the hue that annoys.
We're impossible gods again! Let us dine.

Bill Yarrow

Despondence of the vulgar gods again
annoys that executive taste of bacon
and beans; let us dine on dreaming
that's still impossible while we're
pouring forth emulous sloth, desire,
the seized deed of the fallen body.

The fallen gods of pallid hue...
that vulgar deed in the body that's impossible...
let us dine, let us dine, on executive desire.

Cento of lines from public-domain poems constructed into a sestina, then deconstructed.
- With emulous Taste, that vulgar deed annoys ("Summer Images"), John Clare
- And dreaming Sloth of pallid hue ("Ode for Music"), Thomas Gray
- Despondence seized again the fallen Gods ("Hyperion"), John Keats
- Let us dine on beans and bacon ("The Table and the Chair"), Edward Lear
- Still pouring forth executive desire ("Ode: The Author Apologizes to a Lady, for His being a Little Man"), Christopher Smart
- While we're in the body that's impossible ("The Shadowy Waters"), William Butler Yeats

INVERSIONS OF POUND

Sun-rays of glitter with flour
white with mixed water, wine
sweeter then, and mead; first
speech hurried in, cried I, and
spirit pitiful, dead, impotent,
impetuous... Sat I sternward
from winds and weeping with
heavy shouting with me, about
crowded many: these tender girls,
tears recent with stained souls,
brides of dead, cadaverous Erebus;
unguarded ladder... long the down
going. Came Anticlea then and
companions all lose. Back stepped I.
Odysseus then said, "Mist, close-
webbed, with covered heads, with
mauled many men, sword narrow,
lance bronze: the unsheathed cities
peopled and lands Kimmerian. Coast
dark. Blood dark. The bronze of slain
sheep herds, the slaughtered beasts."
More for men ointment poured. Me
upon pallor canvas, bellying with onward,
out us bore. There men wretched over
stretched night, swartest seas dark over
Neptune, spiteful through return: Elpenor
first spoke and me knew, eyelids dark
with wine abundant and fate ill. This to
come: the nape-nerve, the shattered
buttress. Thou art. How? Heavy, joyless
arms. Dreary wand. Golden his holding.

A poem comprised of lines and phrases taken in reverse order from "Canto I" by Ezra Pound.

Bill Yarrow

Oulipo Casabianca

N+0

The boy stood on the burning deck

N+1

The boycott stood on the burning deckhand

N+2

The boyfriend stood on the burning declaration

N+3

The bra stood on the burning decline

N+4

The brace stood on the burning decongestant

N+5

The bracelet stood on the burning decoration

N+6

The bracket stood on the burning decorator

N+7

The brag stood on the burning decoy

N+8

The braggart stood on the burning decrease

N+9

The braid stood on the burning decree

N+10

The brain stood on the burning dedication

N+11

The brainstorm stood on the burning deduction

N+12

The brainwave stood on the burning deed

N+13

The brake stood on the burning deep

N+14

The bramble stood on the burning defaulter

N+15

The branch stood on the burning defeat

Hart Crane Pantoum No. 2

It is a matter of felicitous juggling
to have the right ones form themselves into the proper pattern at the right mo-
ment.
I am taking a course in advertising
and am perhaps not to be taken seriously.

To have the right ones form themselves into the proper pattern at the right mo-
ment!
Life is meagre with me; I am unsatisfied and left always begging for beauty
and am perhaps not to be taken seriously.
I too have a little toe-nail in the last century.

Life is meagre with me; I am unsatisfied and left always begging for beauty.
In my own work I find the problem of style and form becoming more and more
difficult.
I too have a little toe-nail in the last century
and no amount of will or emotion can help the thing a bit.

In my own work I find the problem of style and form becoming more and more
difficult.
I admit to a slight leaning toward the esoteric
and no amount of will or emotion can help the thing a bit.
The best thing is that the cloud of my father is beginning to move from the
horizon.

I admit to a slight leaning toward the esoteric.
I am fated to a life of parental absorptions.
The best thing is that the cloud of my father is beginning to move from the
horizon.
I met Robert Frost's daughter at a theatre party the other evening.

I am fated to a life of parental absorptions.
I like Marianne Moore in a certain way.
I met Robert Frost's daughter at a theatre party the other evening.
Anything for some money now.

I like Marianne Moore in a certain way.
I am taking a course in advertising.
Anything for some money now.
It is a matter of felicitous juggling.

A pantoum made from lines from *The Letters of Hart Crane 1916-1932*, edited by Brom Weber, University of California Press, Berkeley and Los Angeles, 1965. Out of copyright. Internet Archive.

EDITING INTO OBLIVION

Utopia Parkway (1)
September 20, 2009

"Stand to the side! Stand to the side!"
The policemen usher the loved ones
into an alcove of trees. They are making
room for the ambulance to get through.
There is some bloody business to take
care of. And the sun is thudding hot.

I hate fireworks. Goony-faced loons with
upturned heads staring at pixels of water-
color gunpowder. Explosions inuring us
to the sound of war. The smoky aftertaste
of the googolplex crowd. Lovers encrusted
on sidewalk curbs, embedded in fountains.

I watch the ash float from its catastrophe.
A bumblebee stumbles into my palm.

Bill Yarrow

Utopia Parkway (2)
March 13, 2010

"Stand to the side! Move over! Move over!"
The policemen usher the loved ones
into an alcove of trees. They are making
room for the ambulance to get through.
There is some bloody business to take care
of. There is a slush of people to maintain.

I hate fireworks. Goony-faced loons with
upturned heads staring at pixels of water-
color gunpowder. Explosions inuring us
to the sound of war. The smoky aftertaste
of the googolplex crowd. Lovers encrusted
on sidewalk curbs, embedded in fountains.

I watch the ash float from its catastrophe.
A bumblebee stumbles into my palm.

Utopia Parkway (3)
May 13, 2010

The sun, the sun is thudding hot.
The policemen usher the loved ones
into an alcove of trees. There is some
bloody business to take care of.
There is a slush of people to restrain.

I hate fireworks. Goony-faced loons with
upturned heads staring at pixels of colored
gunpowder. Explosions inuring us to the
acoustics of shooting. The smoky aftertaste
of the complex crowd. Toughs in hoodies.
Lovers flashing gang signs. The history
of dirty loss encrusted on a curb.

I watch ash float from its catastrophe.
A bumblebee stumbles into my palm.

Bill Yarrow

Utopia Parkway (4)
June 25, 2010

The sun, the sun is thudding hot.
The policemen usher the loved ones
into an alcove of trees. There is some
bloody business to take care of.
There is a slush of people to restrain.

I hate fireworks. Goony-faced loons with
upturned heads staring at pixels of colored
gunpowder. Explosions inuring us to the
acoustics of shooting. The smoky taste
of the googolplex crowd. Toughs in sleeveless
hoodies. Lovers flashing gang signs.
The history of dirty loss encrusted on a curb.

As I watch the ash float from its catastrophe,
a bumblebee stumbles into my palm.

Utopia Parkway (5)

August 17, 2010

The sun, the sun is thudding hot.
The policemen usher the loved ones
into an alcove of trees. There is some
bloody business to take care of. *Officer!*
There is a slush of people to restrain.

Who doesn't hate fireworks? Goony-faced
loons with upturned heads staring at pixels
of colored gunpowder. Explosions inuring us
to the acoustics of shooting. The smoky taste
of the googolplex crowd. Toughs in sleeveless
hoodies. Tattooed lovers flashing gang signs.
The history of dirty loss encrusted on a curb.

As we watch the ash float from its catastrophe,
a bumblebee stumbles into the Madonna's palm.

Five versions of "Utopia Parkway."

Bill Yarrow

The Queen of the Underground

❖ Birth is profound, but decay is more profound. Study decay, says the Queen of the Underground.

❖ The sacred body is corrupted and needs to be purged by words, says the Queen of the Underground.

❖ I am the Demon of Release, says the Queen of the Underground.

❖ I am the Mistress of Reveals, says the Queen of the Underground.

❖ I'm currently between religions, says the Queen of the Underground.

❖ I want to see how ugly one can make a poem while still keeping it beautiful, says the Queen of the Underground.

❖ The thirst that can be quenched but not vanquished—that's what I hunger for, says the Queen of the Underground.

❖ Today's editor wants his pound of flash, says the Queen of the Underground.

❖ I know a woman who made a necklace of her child's baby teeth, says the Queen of the Underground.

❖ I am a mere icon, says the Queen of the Underground.

❖ There is no such thing as transitive voice, BUT THERE SHOULD BE, says the Queen of the Underground.

❖ Apple Loan Neon, says the Queen of the Underground.

❖ Diode Niece Scion, says the Queen of the Underground.

❖ I got a telephone in my pajamas, says the Queen of the Underground.

❖ Hurt my eyes open, says the Queen of the Underground.

❖ All bending ends in breaking, says the Queen of the Underground.

❖ Don't be that way, says the Queen of the Underground.

❖   The kitten is in the mail, says the Queen of the Underground.

❖   Fall on your knees, my ass, says the Queen of the Underground.

❖   The Queen of the Underground says, "The Poetry of Bullshit is Dead!"

Flaubert Eats Breakfast with His Mom

they were sitting at the breakfast table
waiting for more toast when she looked
up at him and said your mania for sentences
has dried up your heart that's not true mother
louise did that and gout and the middle
class you're just upset my fruit bowl is empty
come my darling let's take a walk in the garden
and water the desert of my heart the future may
surprise us yet gustave my sun my star
you're incorrigible yes mother I am but
give me your arm the eggs will have to wait
look the sun is bleeding on the flowers the clouds—
soft guardians of virtue— they will protect us
God is out walking his dog while over us
white bees hover like angels of clotted milk

ACKNOWLEDGEMENTS

This volume is more thematic than is usual for me. To that end, I've recycled some poems from my four chapbooks, one from *Wrench* (erbacce press), six from *Fourteen* (OUP), six from *Incompetent Translations and Inept Haiku* (Červená Barva Press), and two from *The Lice of Christ* (MadHat Press). Also one poem is taken from *Pointed Sentences* (BlazeVOX) because I think it fits even better here than it did in that book. I thank all the publishers for permission to republish.

I'd also like to acknowledge and thank the editors and publishers of *After Hours*, *Altered Scale*, *AwkWord Paper Cut*, *Berkeley Poets Cooperative*, *Blue Fifth Review*, *Camroc Press Review*, *Chicago Literati*, *Connotation Press*, *Contrary*, *erbacce*, *Eunoia Review*, *Festival Writer*, *FRiGG*, *Gargoyle*, *Hermeneutics Chaos Literary Journal*, *MadHat*, *Metazen*, *Midstream*, the *Miscreant*, the *Montucky Review*, *Moria*, *New World Writing*, *Novembre*, *OF ZOOS*, *Olentangy Review*, *PANK*, *PoetsArtists*, *RHINO*, *Santa Fe Literary Review*, *Skidrow Penthouse*, *Truck*, *Uno Kudo*, *Wilderness House Literary Review*, *Word Swell*, and the *Zen Space* where others of these poems, some altered in minor or major ways, appeared.

If anything in these poems sounds like an allusion, it is.

Heartfelt thanks to Jane Carman and her team.

Rejected Section Titles

The Time is Out of Blasphemy
Though This Be Blasphemy, yet There is Blasphemy in It
To Put a Blasphemous Disposition On
These Are but Wild and Blasphemous Words
Neither a Blasphemer nor a Blasphemer Be
Your Bait of Blasphemy
O You Must Wear Your Blasphemy with a Difference
Sicklied o'er with a Blasphemous Cast of Thought
By Blasphemy, Find Blasphemy Out
More Blasphemy, and Less Blasphemy
Words without Blasphemy Never to Heaven Go
Too Much of Blasphemy Hast Thou
The Cat Will Mew and Blasphemy Will Have His Day
There's a Blasphemy That Shapes Our Ends

Made in the USA
San Bernardino, CA
29 March 2015